FINDING JOSEPH BRYERS OF THE HOKIANGA

EARLY NEW ZEALAND SETTLER

Dedicated to:

My parents Iris Alfreda Moore and John Sidney Baker and also my cousin Alison Jenkins who with her keen interest and fascination with family origins, encouraged me to pursue this research; and all those descendants of Joseph Bryers of the Hokianga whom I have met over the years and are dedicated to preserving the stories and history of this unique region of New Zealand. We still have much to learn from them.

FINDING JOSEPH BRYERS OF THE HOKIANGA

Early New Zealand Settler

Kenneth M. Baker

2020

Cover: Siege of Ostend (the birthplace of Joseph Brÿers). The three-year siege of the city of Ostend during the Eighty Years' War and the Anglo–Spanish War. Painting by Peter Snayers.
Source: Public Domain, Museum Prinsenhof, Delft.

THE AUTHOR

Dr. Kenneth M. Baker (1944 -), a chemist by training, was born at Auckland, New Zealand and educated at Ellerslie School, Penrose High School[1] and Auckland University where he obtained his M.Sc (Hons) and Ph.D degrees. After being awarded several Research Fellowships he attended Cambridge University where he was a Member of Emmanuel College and carried out post-doctoral research in Chemistry. He went on to become a Syntex Fellow and a Wellcome Foundation Fellow before taking up a corporate management role. He then spent many years in senior management roles in the chemical, pharmaceutical and agriculture industries. He has acted as Chairman of many Business groups, public sector bodies and Government Committees. One of his side interests has always been family history and the First World War. The author resides in Belgium and besides English also speaks the French, Dutch and Italian languages which has proved of great benefit in researching this work.

Dr. Baker is the author of many publications and given many speeches and presentations on science and research, business management, public policy and New Zealand history. He spends his time between Belgium, Italy and New Zealand.

The author is the great-great grandson of Joseph Bryers, the subject of this work.

---

[1] Now One Tree Hill College.

Name Carolus Josephus Brÿers as inscribed on the birth record of Joseph Bryers in 1822 at Ostend, Belgium.

CONTENTS

FOREWARD

Like many other New Zealanders, I have long had an interest in the origins of my family. That is perhaps not unusual given that in the very early days of European migration to the country, most who arrived were leaving their kin for good never to see them again. That was very often a deliberate action. And as a result, memory of heritage was often not passed on within families.

Both my mother's and father's families originated from the Hokianga district of New Zealand. That is not to say my parents were born there, but it meant that the family felt an attachment to this rather magic and relatively isolated area in the Far North of New Zealand.

This particular account is of the origins of one of those antecedents of mine, my great-great-grandfather Joseph Bryers. Within the family, there had always been speculation as to his origin. And many a tale told – true or false. The most frequent was that Joseph was of French heritage - and nothing more than that.

It was not until the early 1960's that I first visited the Hokianga in the company of my parents. They had been married in 1942 and spent their honeymoon visiting the family at Omapere on the South shore of the Hokianga near the Heads. I know little about that event and now it is too late to ask. How they ever got up to the Far North in those days over those largely unformed dusty roads and in the middle of the Second World War, I will never know. I know they visited the signal station at the Hokianga Harbour South Head because we have photographs and they signed the visitors' book. 'Uncle Bill' Bryers was the Signal Master there although I think he did not have much to do during the war except keep an eye out for enemy shipping. The isolated harbour was considered a security risk although protected by its renowned 'bar'.

Based on many years of detailed research, the present account in these pages pulls together what I believe to be a full picture of Joseph Bryers and his origins. The story is about Joseph himself. Other than superficially, no attempt is made to elucidate the lives of his children or further descendants. That is left to others. Many Bryers family members may realise the version recounted herein differs significantly from other popular theories. In these pages and where opportune, an attempt has been made to explain the variation and how the alternative view may have arisen.

It has been my privilege to write this account and I have only been able to do so as a result of my knowledge of European languages and long years of studying and living in Europe. It was a great surprise in later life, for me to learn that I had in fact 'come home' to Belgium.

Kenneth M. Baker
Brussels, Belgium
November 2020

Family of Joseph Bryers (Charles Joseph Bryers) of the Hokianga, Early New Zealand Settler

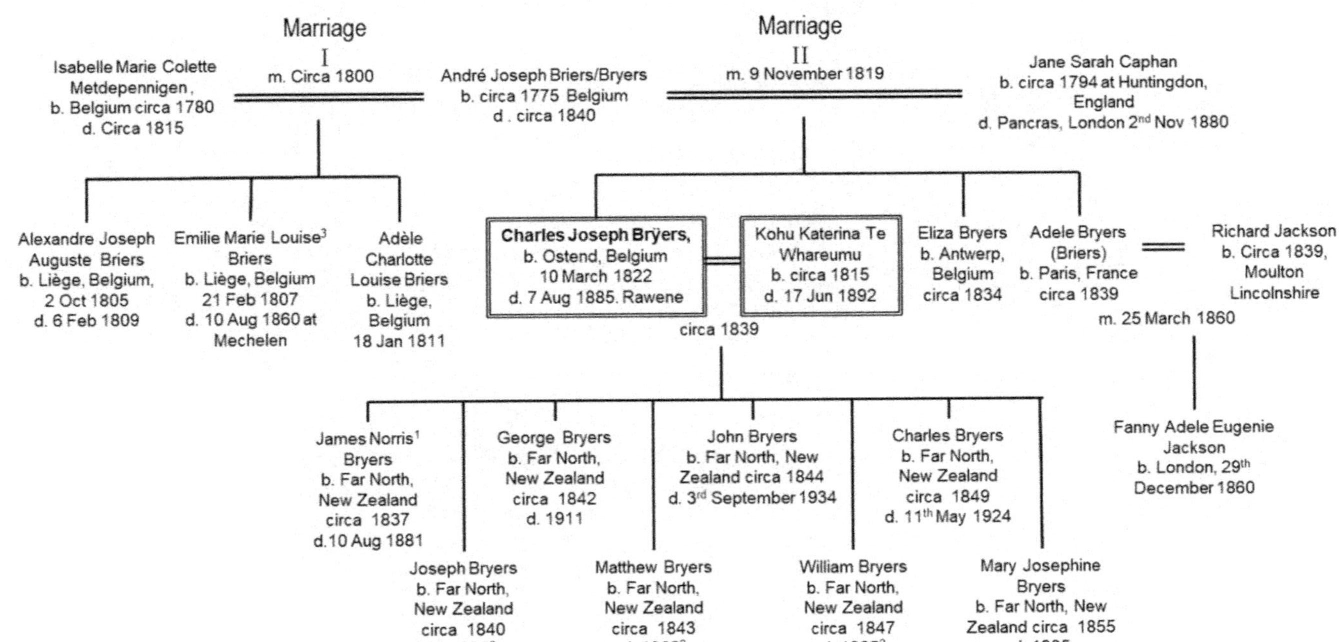

1. James Norris Bryers was almost certainly adopted (taken in) although not formally. His father was likely James Norris who was temporarily in the Bay of islands as a Sea Captain.
2. Died at sea, probably in storms in Cook Straight in late November/early December 1865. Bodies or ship 'Kiwi' never recovered.
3. Death record shows her name as *Emilie Marie Elise Briers* born 24 February 1807.

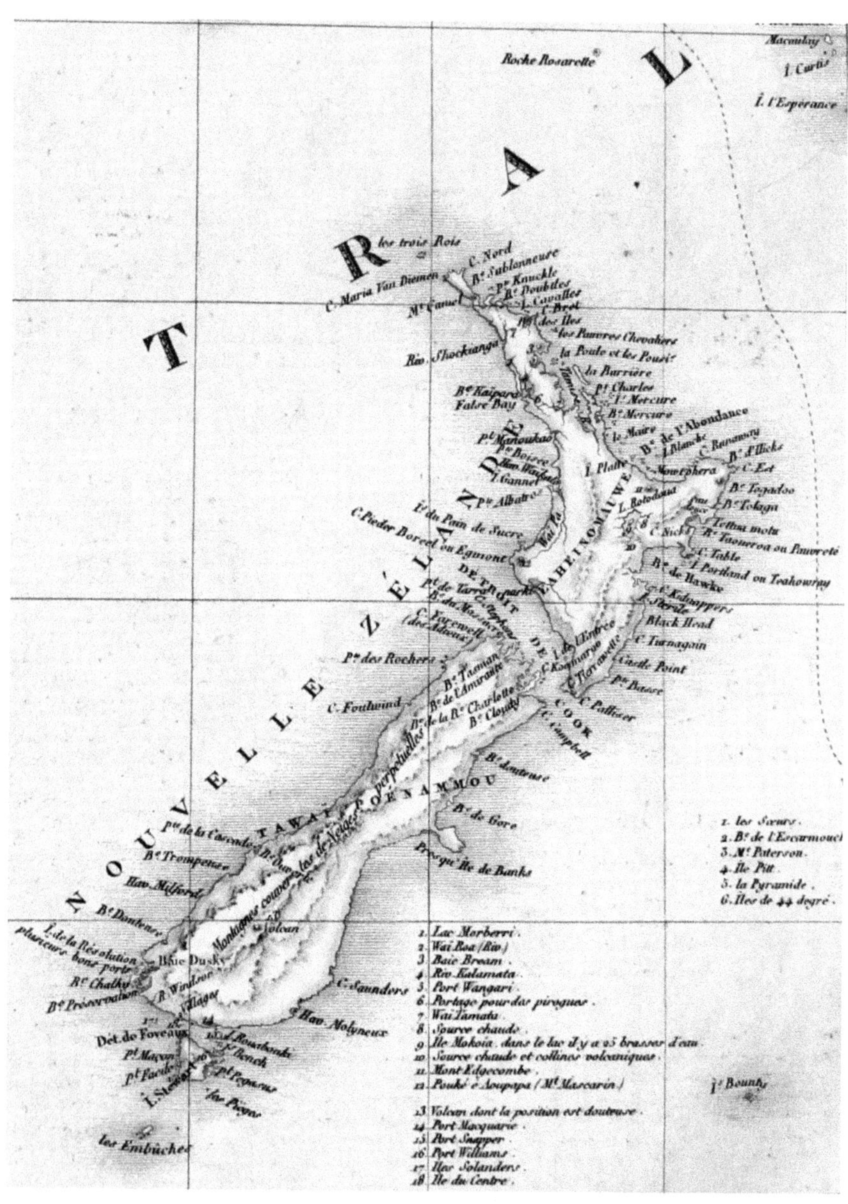

*French Map of New Zealand, 1826 by A. Brué, Geographer to the
King of France. Source: The Author collection*

4

Chapter 1

BIRTHPLACE

On the North Sea coast of Belgium opposite the English Channel ports and Dover lies the ancient fortified port of Ostend with a good and sheltered harbour. From ancient times, Ostend was an important fishing and trading port for the Low Countries and Northern France with England and the Nordic and Baltic countries. Many goods were traded through the port of Ostend including the region's specialty textiles and crops from the fertile lands towards the interior. The town grew rapidly and by the early 1800's was very soon expanding beyond the walls which formed its original fortification. In the 18th century a sheltered inner harbour was created. The port played a major role in the successful Battle of Waterloo in 1815 at which the French Emperor Napoleon was defeated as it was used as a landing place for British troops.

There was regular and varied shipping between London and Ostend in the early 1820's sometimes being twice or thrice a week. The traffic would have been for the most part traded goods.

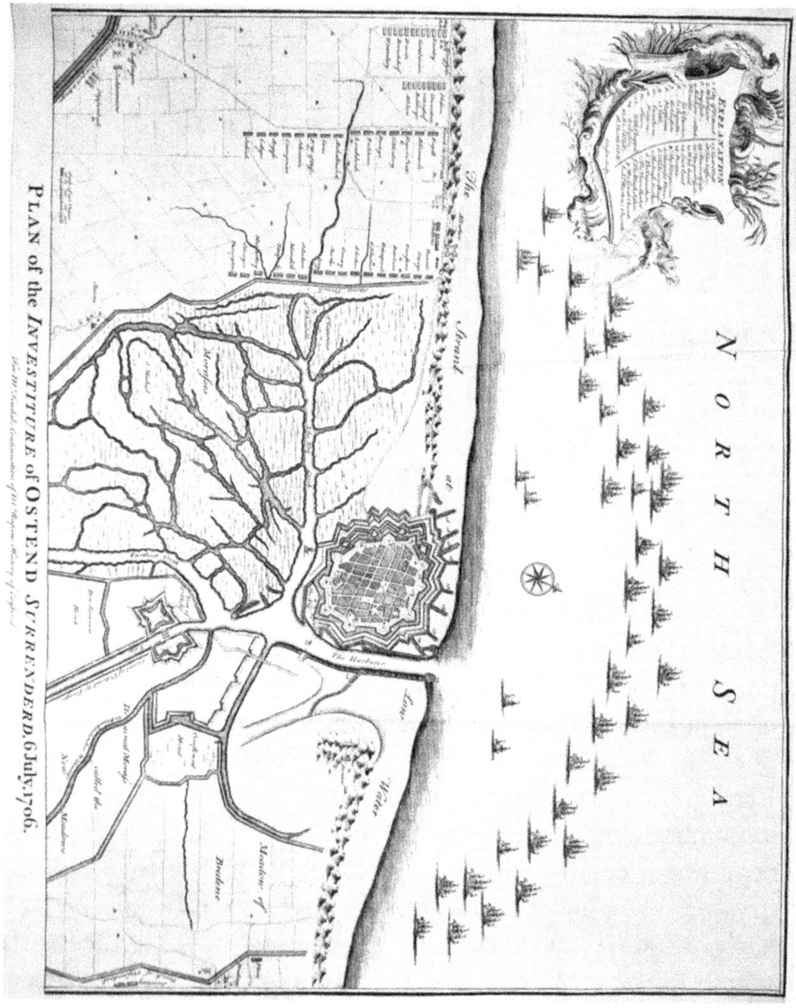

Map of the ancient fortress of Ostend 1706. Source: Collection, the author.

Disembark-ation of British Troops at Ostend circa 1815 in anticipation of the Battle of Waterloo. Source: Collection, the Author

In early March 1822, the weather across Northern France, Belgium and all the way up to North Holland was atrocious. Severe electrical storms had ravaged the region and country towns and villages. The weather had been sufficiently dramatic that most European and English newspapers[2,3] of the day carried reports that on Saturday the 9th March, at Stijl on the south-west outskirts of Ostend, lightning had struck the church tower and the church had burned to the ground. For some reason this event was considered sensational and noteworthy whereas in today's world this would hardly have made the international press.

A later ship, the 'Aquila' steam-ship leaving Antwerp for London as part of a new regular shipping service in 1854. Source: Collection the author, Illustrated London News, 30 September 1854.

Amid all this weather pandemonium, the vessel *The Prince of Waterloo* had sailed from London to Ostend[4]. The ship was no doubt named in honour of the victory of the Anglo-Allied armies under the Duke of Wellington over Napoleon at the Battle of Waterloo in 1815 and was likely

---

[2] *Journal de Belgique, 13 March 1822 (in French).*
[3] *Star (London), 18 March 1822.*
[4] *Public Ledger and Daily Advertiser, London, 14 March 1822.*

to be no more than a few years old.   At this period, every ship and mariners set off literally, in the hands of God and were condemned to take whatever the heavens delivered. Even primitive weather forecasting did not arrive in Europe until the mid-1850's.   Inevitably, the rough weather was probably partly if not completely responsible for the events which followed and are reported in this account.

It came to pass that early on the cold and blustery late winter's day of Monday, 11th March 1822 at the coastal port of Ostend in the Flanders Region of the Low Countries in what is now Belgium, a visiting London merchant left his wife behind at their lodgings in the town and walked to the Town Hall in the centre of the old fortified settlement. That merchant was the forty five year old Andreas Josephus (André Joseph) Brÿers[5], pronounced Bryers in English who was about to register the birth of his son Carolus Josephus (Charles Joseph) who had been born in the same town at ten o'clock the previous evening.   His twenty-two year old wife Joanna Sarah[6] (Jane Sarah) Capham had been attended by the fifty-year old local surgeon, Petrus (Pieter) Malpast. Why a young lady in the last stages of pregnancy had ventured on such a voyage across the Channel remains unknown but it probably had something do to with the urgency of a commercial deal by her husband. On his walk to the Town Hall, Joseph Bryers was accompanied by the surgeon and they presented themselves to Thomas Hamman Dekeyn who, acting for the Ostend burgomaster, registered the birth of the child with as witnesses, Malpast and another, a twenty-seven year old local shopkeeper, Franciscus (Francis) Eenvard. Joseph Bryers the elder signed himself *"Bryers"*.

---

[5] As inscribed in the town population registers.
[6] As inscribed in the town population registers.

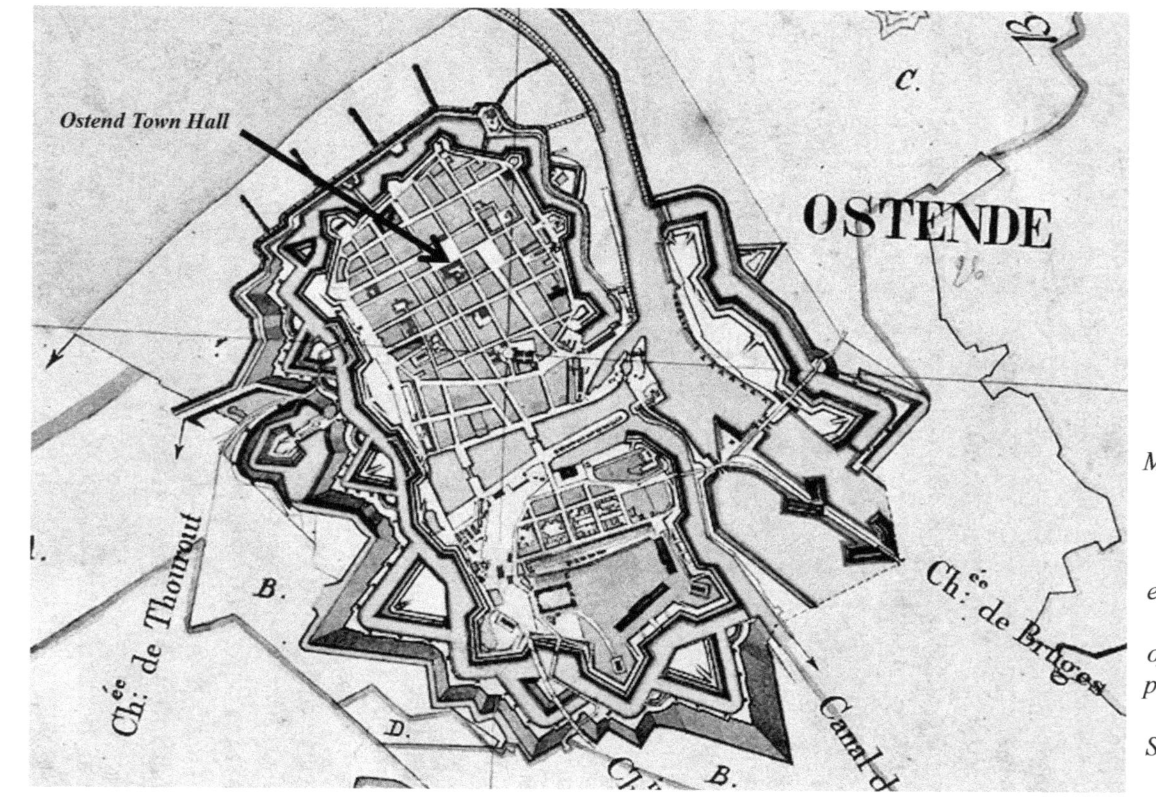

Map c. 1820, of the port of Ostend showing the extensions and creation of the new and protected inner harbour.
Source: Public domain

The Town Hall Ostend, Belgium, originally constructed 1709. Source: Author collection

The original Town Hall of Ostend was built in 1709 and it was to last until 1940 when during the Second World War, Ostend came under sustained aerial attack beginning 19 May 1940. During the night of 27 May 1940 the city's original Town Hall that was burned down. Most of the historic building and the whole of the Ostend City archive was destroyed in the fire.

Some explanation and interpretation is required of the above facts and names. Ostend by the early 1820's was very international being at the crossroads of intercontinental trading, arguably the region being the largest trading centre in the world at the time. Many languages were spoken, the most widely being Dutch, English and French.

Although the French language was often used and was the language of the upper classes, as can be observed in the birth registration for Charles Joseph Brÿers, the population registers in 1822 were written in the Dutch language. And as a consequence of the earlier introduction of the Napoleonic civil code, Christian names were mostly recorded in their Latin equivalents. Thus the father whose Christian names in daily life were *André Joseph* and always referred to as 'Joseph' was recorded as Andreas Josephus while the new-born son *Charles Joseph* was registered as Carolus Josephus. The young lady who had given birth was recorded as Joanna Sarah, the Latin form of *Jane Sarah Capham* with as was convention, her maiden name being recorded. Making for more complications, the father's surname was registered in the phonetic fashion as *Brÿers*, i.e. duplicating in Dutch the oral sound with the peculiar "long i" of Dutch and thus pronounced Bryers in English. Considerable future confusion was to result of these variations in spellings of the written name.

Andreas Josephus Brÿers and his wife Joanna Sarah were recorded as normally residing in London. Although there is no way of knowing definitively, it is highly probable that Brÿers and his wife had arrived at Ostend aboard the *Prince of Waterloo* after a very rough passage, not ideal conditions for a young woman in the advanced stages of pregnancy.   By the 1830's the town contained at least nine hotels a large number for its size but reflecting the number of merchants and traders who passed through. That number included the Hotel de la Cour Imperiale, the Hotel du Lion d'Or, the Ship Hotel and the Hotel d'Allemagne.   There were also consulates from England, Denmark, France, a number of German States, the Netherlands and Prussia, all of which demonstrated the commercial importance of the town.   To further mark the influence of the British, besides the normal Catholic churches the town also housed an Anglican church.

In conclusion, the Joseph Bryers who eventually went to reside on the Hokianga in New Zealand was born at Ostend Belgium on the 10th March 1822 and given the name Charles Joseph Brÿers by his parents André Joseph Briers, a Belgian and his wife Jane Capham an English lady from Huntingdon.

Both the young Charles Joseph and his father André Joseph were in future, both to be more commonly known by their second Christian name, Joseph.

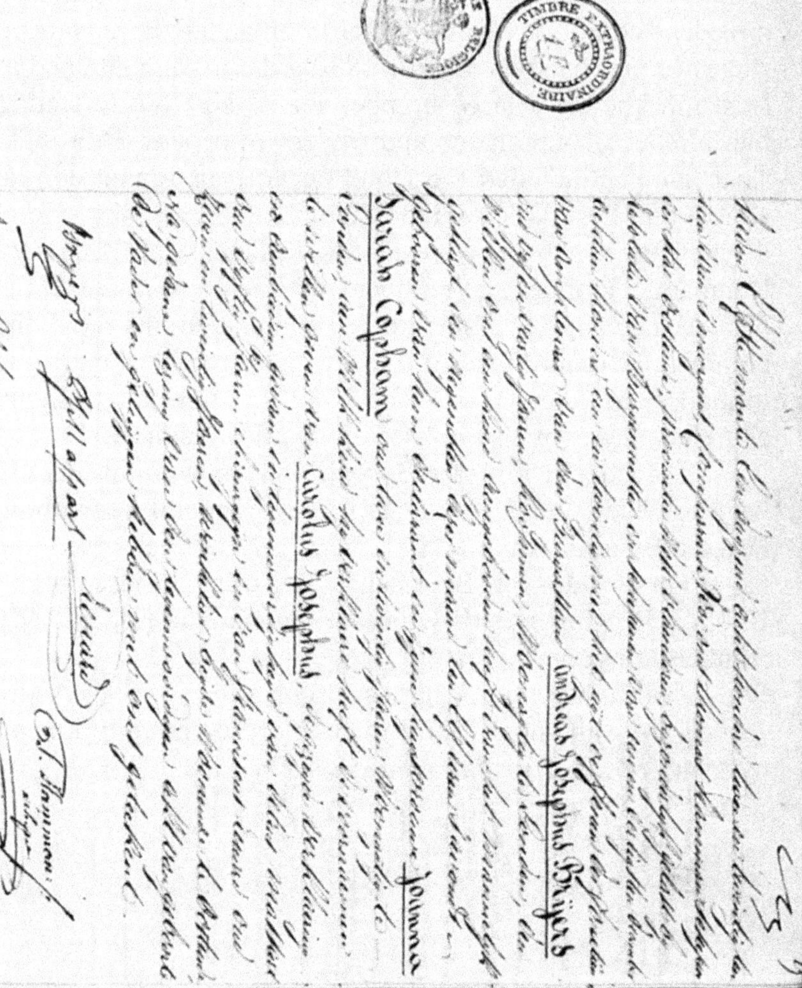

Birth record at
Ostend, Belgium
of
Charles Joseph
Bryers, 10 March
1822

Chapter 2

JOSEPH BRYERS & JANE CAPHAM

By the time young Joseph was born, the Bryers couple had been married about two years. The marriage registers of St James Church, Piccadilly, Westminster, London, record that Joseph Bryers and Jane Capham had been married by Banns on the 9th November 1819. The celebrations had been conducted by the preacher J. E. Maddy and the witnesses were James Skaller and Mary Baxter, both very likely to have been parishioners and not necessarily known to the happy couple. Banns are the public announcement in a Christian parish church or in the town council of an impending marriage between two specified persons and are mostly associated with the Catholic Church, the Church of England, and the Church of Sweden and denominations of similar traditions. The purpose of Banns is to enable anyone to raise any justified concerns so as to prevent invalid marriages. Such concerns vary but could normally include lack of parental consent,

Page

MARRIAGES solemnized in the Parish of **SAINT JAMES, WESTMINSTER,**
in the County of Middlesex, in the Year 1819.

_____________________ of ___ Parish

and _____________________ of ___ Parish

were Married in this Church by _______ with Consent of _______________

this _______ Day of ___________ in the Year One Thousand Eight Hundred and **Nineteen.**

By me, _________________________

This Marriage was solemnized between us, { _________________________

In the Presence of { _________________________

No. ___

a continuing pre-existing marriage or the couple's being related within the prohibited degrees of kinship. According to Church law, the marriage should be celebrated in the parish where at least one of the parties was resident.

Interior of St James Church, Westminster, c. 1806.
Source: Unknown Author, Public Domain

Given the age difference between the pair and other circumstances, as will be seen later it is also highly likely that no active parental consent had been forthcoming for the marriage of James Bryers and Jane Caphan, probably because the parents were not made aware.

St James Church Picadilly mid-1800's. Source: St James Church

St James Church, Westminster where the couple were married is an Anglican Church located on Picadilly in central London. The church is a wonderful example of the architectural work of Sir Christopher Wren. In 1662, Henry Jermyn, 1st Earl of St Albans, was granted land for residential development on what was then the outskirts of London. He set aside land for the building of a parish church and churchyard on the south side of what is now Piccadilly. Christopher Wren was appointed the architect in 1672 and the church was consecrated on 13 July 1684 by Henry Compton, the Bishop of London. In 1685 the parish of St James was created for the church. The church was severely damaged by enemy action in 1940, during the Second World War. This church is also famous as being the place where Oliver Cromwell was baptised in 1599.

The south and east front of St James's Church, Piccadilly,
London published 1814. Source: Public Domain

Jane Capham was born at or near Huntingdon to the north-west of Cambridge in about 1800 according to her listing as Jane Bryers in the 1851 census of England. The surname Capham is rather unusual and many references to the Capham name are found in this district. Although there is no exact reference to her birth, it is possible Jane was related to Rachel Capham who also according to the 1851 census was a widowed small shop keeper in St Mary's Parish, Huntingdon and who had been born in the same town. Alternatively she may have been the daughter of John Capham, and his wife Eleanor also of Huntingdon. John was a cordwainer[7] of the All Saints and St John Parish, Huntingdon and they had three other children, Mary, born 3 August 1803, William, born 8 January 1806 and Catharine, born 4 November 1808.

Joseph Bryers, husband of Jane Capham was a considerably more complex character. He was born André Joseph Briers somewhere in the period 1775 to 1776, almost certainly at Liège, Belgium. There are no available remaining birth records for this period. He was thus French speaking however inevitably he also spoke Dutch given the nature of his business as a trader, the closeness to Holland and other factors such as where he traded and the family into which he married. Prior to his marriage to Jane Capham he had been previously married to a lady named Isabelle Marie Colette Metdepennigen[8] who was possibly from the district around Mechelen (Malines in French) in the province of Antwerp. Little is known of her and no marriage record has yet been found although the marriage certainly took place during the period of the French Republican calendar in the early 1800's. The couple were comfortably off and resided at the rue Derrière St Jacques[9] No. 483, in the south quarter of the town of Liège in what appears to have been a substantial building also occupied by Mr. Fourcault a gentleman of independent means and probably the owner. This district of Liège was clearly inhabited by the independently well-off and besides traders also included prominent lawyers[10].

---

[7] Maker of shoes from new leather.

[8] There are many variations on this name such as 'Mettepennignen' and even 'Met De Penningen' which makes searching the family very difficult.

[9] Since re-named rue Rouveroy, Liège.

[10] Bulletin de l'Institut Archéologique Liègeois, Tome LXIX, 1952 Edité avec le concours du Gouvernement, Maison Curtius, Liège.

View circa 1850 of the Derrière St Jacques Quarter of Liège. The Briers family lived in the houses to the left in the vicinity of the small arched bridge. Source: Collection, the Author.

21

Rue Derrière St Jacques, Liège circa 1900 - Houses in the vicinity of the Briers residence. Source: Collection, the Author.

Contemporary view of the Liege and the Meuse River circa 1840. Source: Collection the author

While resident in the Derrière St Jacques Quarter,
Isabelle bore Joseph at least three children:

- *Alexandre Joseph Auguste Briers*, born at Liège, 2nd
  October 1805 (*13th day of the month of Vendémiaire
  in the year 14 of the French Republic – calendar in
  use at the time*).
- *Emilie Marie Louise Briers*, born at Liège, 21st
  February 1807.
- *Adèle Charlotte Louise Briers*, born at Liège, 18th
  January 1811.

Their first child, Alexandre, was to die at the early age
of three on the 6th February 1809.

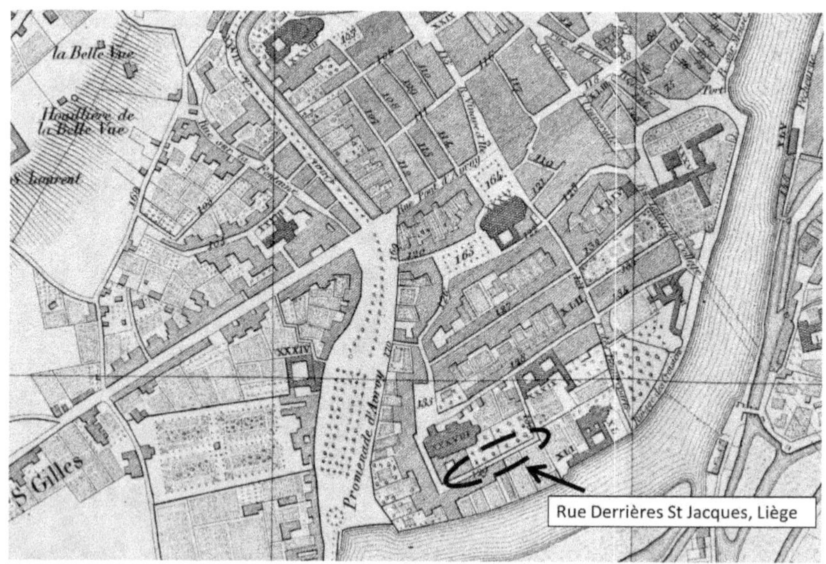

*Location of rue Derrière St Jacques, Liège near the river on a map
circa 1820. Source: Collection the author*

Joseph was recorded as a 'negociant', a merchant
and indications are that he was in textiles, probably
woollens and linens and was likely to have travelled

widely. He was known to have a commercial relationship with a Jean-Nicolas David at Francomot a manufacturer of bedclothes and sheets[11] located near Ensival in the region of Verviers.

The Liège Region was the birthplace of the industrial revolution on the continent, notably due to the abundant coal mines in the district. The manufacturing staple at the time was the processing of wool and woollen goods in contrast to the area nearer the coast around Bruges which was famous for linens.

Joseph Briers' notoriety did not end with his commercial activities and he was to become noteworthy for the role his personal circumstances played in setting jurisprudence in the Kingdom of the Netherlands of which Belgium was a part until the revolution of 1830[12].

On the 6th October 1815, the Commercial Court of Liège in his absence had declared André Joseph Briers a 'fraudulent bankrupt'. The size of the adjudged fraud was judged to be 281,000 francs[13], a very substantial sum. Briers had probably got wind of the probable court action and had fled, and it can now be assumed that his destination was most probably London. In 1817, the High Court at Liège condemned Briers in absentia to twenty years hard labour and a period in the stocks (public exhibition). Evidently, Briers still had wealthy family in Liège because they made a financial arrangement with the creditors in 1824 and which indicates the family was still in touch with each other during this period. As evidenced by the birth of

---

[11] *Inventaire des archives de l'entreprise textile Jean-Nicolas David à Francomont, 1685-1850*; State Archives of Belgium.

[12] *Pasicrisie ou Receuil Générale de la Jurisprudence des Cours de France et de Belgique*, 1814-1840, Bruxelles, 1849. p. 6, Banqueroute Frauduleuse.

[13] It is extremely difficult to calculate the value of 281,000 francs in today's terms but it would have been of the order of one million dollars now (2020).

his son at Ostend in 1822, Briers, or Bryers as he now called himself, had started to trade again from his base in London to his old bailiwick on the continent.

Traders at the Antwerp Bourse 1858. Source: Collection the author, Illustrated London News, 21 August 1858

Clearly Briers continued to carry on his trade on the continent including in Belgium, even though he was taking a risk and still being pursued by the State authorities for evasion. Even in those days, the law was diligent in catching up with miscreants. Briers was arrested in Antwerp in 1827 and then brought back to be imprisoned at Liège. As a result, Briers and his lawyers filed an appeal based on a technicality, that of the authorities not having published the initial judgement. Further, when the case was re-heard at the High Court on the 7th January 1828 and having heard the arguments of Brier's lawyers, Teste, Dereux et Forgeur, the public prosecutor declared the accusations against Briers inadmissible as he had never been in bankruptcy. In other words, the court had concluded that the charges had no basis in law. A trader could not be fraudulent bankrupt. Thus the appeal was upheld.

No further information is available and it must be assumed that Briers was released from prison and was a free man once again. Now a free man, he was free to return to London and carry out his business. The later evidence suggests he did not return to London and remained on the continent which had serious consequences for his son Joseph Bryers.

Chapter 3

JOSEPH BRYERS EARLY YEARS

Joseph Bryers junior had been born at Ostend Belgium in early 1822 at the time his mother Jane was travelling with his father André Joseph on the continent for business reasons. Evidently as is now known, his father was also escaping justice and so was taking a high risk even being present in Belgium. Travelling with a small baby was no small chore in those days given the modes of transport and the rough conditions of the roads, especially in winter. Inevitably they would have been able to visit family which would have partly alleviated the difficulties for even part of the time.

Although they had been married in London, the family appeared to spend the majority of their time in Belgium and probably also nearby France where most of the centres of the linen textile production industry were located. At some time, probably in early 1826, Jane and Joseph senior decided that carrying on business as a textiles

29

trader throughout Europe, avoiding pursuit as a wanted man while managing a small growing child. Even if the young child could be left with relatives in Belgium for a short time, it was not viable proposition. And so the hunt was on for an appropriate place to lodge the child and where he would also receive an education in the English language rather than the French-speaking environment to which the child had become accustomed.

In England, there were the traditional boarding schools such as Eton, Rugby and Harrow. However these were not to Joseph's taste and besides being very expensive, he probably considered were somewhat too English. Inevitably they consulted family and friends, particularly in the French Flanders Region on the continent who had a similar issue and eventually they settled on a Catholic school at Sedgley Park near Wolverhampton. Sedgley Park was some one hundred kilometres west of Jane's hometown of Huntingdon. A possible source of advice was those who had some familiarity with what had been a prominent and well-established Catholic boarding school, the English College at Douay[14] in France close to the Belgian border. Douay was in the region where Bryers would have visited regularly for his textiles business being a production source for linen. The school selected for young Joseph, Sedgley Park School, was established in 1762 and for which Douay had been somewhat of a model. The school at Douay however, had been closed since 1793 just after and as a result of the French Revolution. It should also be recalled that following the Catholic faith in England was not easy, forbidden for many years, and holding of any public office by a Catholic was proscribed. A tiny number of those laws still exist today and are even now to this day being struck from the law-books. Receiving a Catholic education in England was also very

---

[14] Modern-day spelling, *Douai*.

difficult and dangerous although the first steps, encouraged by Bishop Challoner[15], were taken in 1760 to establish a Catholic school for girls. In 1705, Challoner had been sent on a sort of scholarship to be educated at the English College at Douay, France. Challoner entered the English College there on the 29 July. He was to remain at Douay for the next twenty-five years there, first as student, then as professor, and lastly as Vice-President of the parent University of Douay.

The success of the girls' school led to Challoner then inspiring the Rev William Errington to successfully open another trial school for boys at Betley, Staffordshire, in January 1762[16] at near Newcastle-Under-Lyme on the border with Cheshire.   The small school numbering some eighteen scholars was not to remain there for long and on Lady Day, the 25 March 1763, after a journey accomplished in a covered wagon, the boys and teachers arrived at Sedgely Park from Betley. Challoner's intention had been that boys who had been educated at Sedgley Park School would later go on to complete their education at his old school at Douay in France. Some did, but after the French Revolution, this was no longer possible following the closing of the French school. The original eighteen scholars at Sedgley Park are listed below although it seems not all eighteen removed to Sedgley Park[17]. Looking at the entry dates for the boys, it can be said the recruitment of the scholars was very slow in the beginning.

---

[15] Richard Challoner (1691–1781) was an English Roman
Catholic bishop, a leading figure of English Catholicism during the greater part of the 18th century. The titular Bishop of Doberus, he is perhaps most famous for his revision of the Douay–Rheims translation of the Bible.

[16] The History of Cotton College at Sedgley park, 1761-1873, at
Cotton, 1875-, by Rev. Canon W. Buscot, Burns Oates & Washbourne Ltd., London, 1940.

[17] *The History of Sedgley Park School, Staffordshire*, by F.C.
Husenbeth, D.D., Richardson and Son, London, 1856.

1762	January	9	Charles FLINN, evidently the first scholar
		24	Francis HALFORD
		24	James LEIGH
	February	12	James POTIER
		12	Charles POTIER
	March	13	James EDWARDS
		13	William OSBORN
	June	28	John Baptist SLATE
	July	16	James EDWARDS, Jun.
		26	Bryan GORMOND
	August	26	Edward JONES
		29	Joseph OLIVIER
	September	17	Thomas PICKERING
	October	28	Thomas WEST, *al.* HARRISON
		28	James SNOWDON
1763	January	19	Hamilton CANFIELD
		19	John PULLEN
		19	James TASKER

The original purpose Challoner had when opening the school was to provide a Catholic education for the young sons of the aristocracy and gentry up to the age of twelve. When they were old enough, the intention was they would pass on to one or other of the English Colleges on the continent. In practice, many had gone on to Douay. The specific purpose of establishing the school at Sedgley Park was to enable the middle classes who could not afford to send their sons to colleges abroad, for them to receive a complete secondary education in England. A certain number of the gentry also placed their boys at Sedgeley and if as usual a higher pension was paid, they were received as 'parlour-boarders'. A parlour boarder is an archaic term for a privileged category of pupil at a boarding school and can be described as paying more than the other pupils, in return for which they got a room of their own. A parlour was a small reception room, from the French *"parler"*, implying a place for quiet conversation.

In today's terms, the daily school programme seems very onerous and rigid. Every day, the boys got up at six o'clock, dressed, and when the master gave the word to "kneel down," one boy recited aloud the "Our Father," "Hail Mary", Apostles' Creed, "Confiteor," and Acts of Faith, Hope, Love of God, Love of our Neighbour and Contrition, concluding with short prayers to our Blessed Lady, our Guardian Angel, and all the Saints. After that they rushed down stairs to wash and play until quarter to seven when they went to Catechism in the Playroom till the bell rang for Mass at half-past seven. Chapel was followed by breakfast, and then study until twelve with a break of fifteen minutes playtime at ten o'clock. A half-hour lunch was served at a quarter past twelve by the master opening the Refectory door.   This was followed by playtime until two and then study until six except for a break at four o'clock when each boy was given a piece of bread called 'four o'clock' and allowed a glass of water. The evening meal was served at six followed by play time until quarter to eight after which followed chapel for Night Prayers and then bed. Each boy knelt at his bed, and said his prayers to himself before going to sleep. On Tuesdays and Thursdays, the afternoons were playtime but at times those who asked to be able to 'study' were allowed and were able to separate and study, write or draw.

On Sundays and Holidays the programme was catechism at a quarter-past seven, mass at eight, public spiritual reading after breakfast for half-an-hour, then play until dinner. Boys had time in chapel for private devotion or spiritual reading and all was followed by further play time until Vespers at three o'clock followed by play until supper at six and again free until eight after which was prayers and bed. In retrospect, it can be said that all this was a truly heavy load for young boys none of whom was older than ten.

Boys were generally supplied with a basic set of clothing which was included in the pension costs although parents were free to provide the boys with their own clothing. In the latter case, the quality of clothing worn by the boys was invariably much better. The school also possessed a resident tailor for repairing the boys' clothes and also a cobbler to mend shoes.

From the records, the young Joseph Bryers was known to be attending Sedgley Park School from around April 1826 until March 1829. At that time the school roll was about 110.

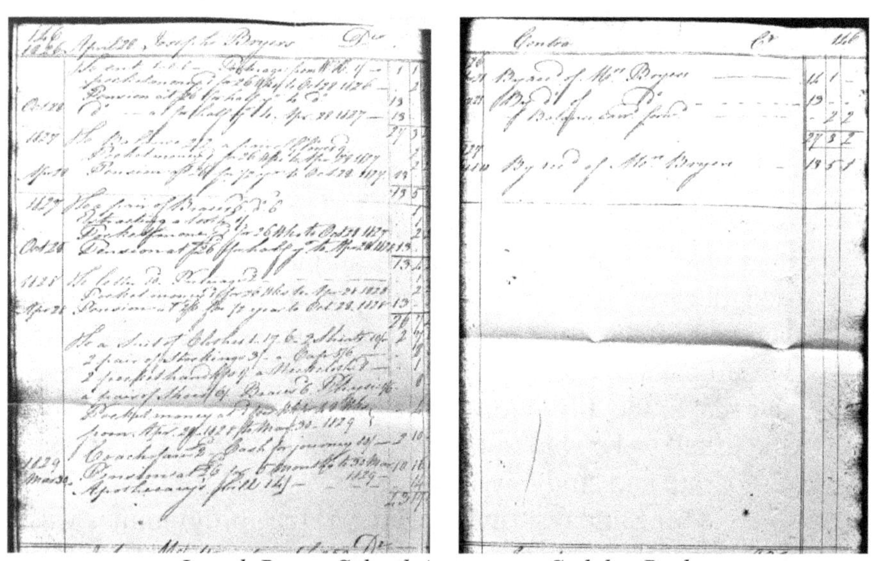

Joseph Bryers School Accounts at Sedgley Park.
Invoices were addressed to Mrs Bryers
(see transcription below)

Date	Dr.	£	s	d	Date	Contra	Cr.	£	s	d
1826, April 28, Joseph Bryers,										
	To: ent. £ 1.0.0. Portage from Wolverhampton 1/-	1	1	-	April 28	By receipt of Mrs Bryers		14	1	-
	Pocket money 1d for 26 weeks to October 28, 1826 –		2	2						
	Pension at £26 for half year to October 28, 1826.	13	-	-						
Oct. 28	Pension at £26 for half year to April 28, 1827.	13	-	-		By receipt of Mrs Bryers		13	-	-
						Balance carried forward		-	2	2
		27	3	2				27	3	2
1827	To: Balance 2/2 a pair of gloves at 9d.		2	11						
	Pocket money for 26 weeks to April 28, 1827		2	2						
April 28	Pension at £26 for half year to October 28, 1827.	13	-	-						
		13	5	1		By receipt of Mrs Bryers		13	5	1
1827	To: pair of braces at 6d do. 6d		1	-						
	Extraction of tooth 1/-		1	-						
	Pocket money for 26 weeks to October 28, 1827		2	2						
Oct 28	Pension at £26 for half year to April 28, 1828	13	4	2						
1828	To: Letter 10d, postage 2d		1	2						
	Pocket money for 26 weeks to April 28, 1828		2	2						
April 28	Pension at £26 for half year to October 28, 1828	13	-	-						
		26	7	4						
	To: A suit of clothes 1..17.6; 2 shirts 10/-	2	7	6						
	2 pairs stocking 3/-; a cap 5/6		8	6						
	2 pocket handerkerchiefs 1/- ; a neck collar 8d		1	8						
	A pair of shoes 6/-; Braces 6d; Physic 1/6		8	-						
	Pocket money at 1d per week for 48 weeks from April 28, 1828 to March 30, 1829.		4	-						
1829	Coach fare £2, cash for journey 10/-		2	10						
March 30	Pension at £26 for 5 months to 30 march 1829	10	16	8						
	Apothecary's bills 14/-		14	-						
		43	17	6						

Transcrition of Joseph Bryers School Accounts at Sedgley Park 1826-1829.
(Invoices were addressed to Mrs Bryers)

Sedgley Park School, 1826, as depicted in the work The History of Cotton College at Sedgley park, 1761-1873, at Cotton, 1875-, *by Rev. Canon W. Buscot. Source: Collection The Author.*

Of interest is the detail of Joseph Bryers' school account (including accounting errors) which unusually was addressed to Mrs Bryers and not his father. This can possibly be explained by Joseph Bryers senior, because he was on the run from the law in Belgium, not wanting to reveal his location or even that he was still alive. Young Joseph's mother Jane Bryers was thus recorded as responsible for, and paid for his schooling. Joseph's mother Mrs. Bryers was charged one shilling[18] for transporting the boy from Wolverhampton to the school at Sedgley Park. From this it can be deduced that Joseph had travelled by coach probably from London to Wolverhampton the closest large coach town to Sedgley Park School, on one of the regular Birmingham coaches likely to have been the *Union*[19] which left London at quarter to five in the evening. The journey of some 200 kilometres and would have taken several days at a cost of some two pounds[20]. The coaches called at St Albans, Dunstable and Coventry.

As the following extract[21] describes, travelling by coach was a dangerous business even though the speed was no more than ten or eleven kilometres per hour.

"One of the more serious among coach accidents was that which befell the London and Dorking stage, in April 1826. It was one of those coaches that did not carry a guard. It left the "Elephant and Castle" at nine o'clock in the morning, full inside and out, and arrived safely at Ewell, where Joseph Walker, who was both coachman and proprietor, alighted for the purpose of getting a parcel

---

[18] About nine New Zealand Dollars in today's money (2020).

[19] Pigot's London Directory.

[20] About three hundred and fifty New Zealand Dollars in today's money (2020).

[21] *Stage-Coach and Mail in Days of Yore. A Picturesque History of the Coaching Age, Vol II*, Charles G. Harper, Chapman and Hall Ltd., London, 1903 (See The Project Gutenberg EBook)

from the hind boot. He gave the reins to a boy who sat on the box, and all would have been well had it not been for the thoughtless act of the boy himself, who cracked the whip, and set the horses off at full speed. They dashed down the awkwardly curving road by the church and into a line of wooden railings, which were torn down for a length of twelve yards. Coming then to some immovable obstacle, the coach was violently upset, and the whole of the passengers hurled from the roof. All were seriously injured, and one was killed. This unfortunate person was a woman, who fell upon some spiked iron railings, "which," says the contemporary account, "entered her breast and neck. She was dreadfully mutilated, none of her features being distinguishable. She lingered until the following day, when she expired in the greatest agony." The gravestone of this unfortunate person is still to be seen in the leafy churchyard of Ewell, inscribed to the memory of "Catherine, wife of James Bailey, who, in consequence of the overturning of the Dorking Coach, April 1826, met with her death in the 22nd year of her age.""

Travelling From London to Wolverhampton alone for a four year old boy seems rather daunting. For the price paid it is unlikely he had anybody such as servant accompanying him although at the price he would probably have sat *'inside'*. There is also another charge of two pounds for a coach fare in early 1829 with spending money for the journey of ten shillings which seems to indicate that he may have visited family although further conclusions cannot be drawn. The cost of his schooling at 52 pounds per year, a hefty sum in those days[22], indicates that Joseph was probably a Parlour Boarder, most likely because of his age which would have been two or three years younger than the other boys.

---

[22] Estimated to be at least 20,000 New Zealand Dollars in 2020.

Red Rover Southampton Stage Coach circa 1820. Source Alamy

However the most revealing thing about the school accounts is that in mid-1827, Mrs Bryers apparently stopped paying for her son's schooling and she and his father André Joseph Bryers seem to have abandoned the child at Sedgley Park School. It is known from the various legal proceedings that in 1827, André Joseph Bryers was arrested in Antwerp. Jane Bryers his wife was almost certainly in Antwerp at the time as well and would have been at her wits end and without a source of funds or other means of support. And following Joseph Bryers Senior's imminent release from his legal constraints, he was unlikely to return to London. Meanwhile, back at Sedgley Park School, young Joseph went from being a 'parlour boy' to an ordinary student supported by the school funds. That the school bought and paid for new clothing supports this theory, even if re-payment was not forthcoming from Joseph's parents.

Even though Joseph's father, André Joseph Bryers was acquitted of all accusations of fraud in 1828, there is little evidence that young Joseph returned to the family fold, either in London or Belgium, if ever. In the absence of any solid proof, it may also be speculated that young Joseph had been withdrawn from school during 1828 or 1829, without the school accounts being settled, and sent to live with the family in Liège, in a French-speaking environment. There he would speak English with his mother and French with almost everyone else. A clue to origins could have been had from the regional accent or dialect with which Joseph spoke French. However it is almost certainly true that those he encountered in New Zealand would not have had sufficient familiarity with the language to be able to determine this.

The evidence of a happy home life is rather to the contrary. The period at Sedgely Park School was likely to have been the most stable in young Joseph's life. It appears that Joseph left Sedgeley Park School early in 1829 or 1830, destination unknown. He would have been just eight years old at the time.

That Joseph enjoyed his period at Sedgeley Park School and felt it was in a sense 'family' and that he had a sense of belonging and a home, can be gleaned from a newspaper notice Joseph placed in New Zealand many years later in 1868[23]. This was the occasion of the marriage of his son Charles in Auckland. The notice reads *"On March 24 (1868), at St. Paul's Church by the Rev. Archdeacon Lloyd, Charles, youngest son of Joseph Bryers, late of Sedgley Park, Staffordshire, England, to Mary Ann Constant (Constance), eldest daughter of the late Zedbury (Sedborough) Mayne, Ensign, late of the 58th Regiment – Home papers please copy"*.

Clearly Joseph felt the school and the friends he had made there were the most important people from his former life on what was now the other side of the world. This can only be interpreted as Joseph being estranged from his

---

[23] *Daily Southern Cross,* Auckland, March 1868

parents and birth family, an interpretation cemented by the fact that he seems to have never passed on accurately his mother's first name and especially in writing. Recording of family data was never necessary or obligatory in pre-colonial New Zealand. In later life in New Zealand, Joseph never talked much of his earlier life and that combined with his childrens' and grandchildrens' inability to remember accurately what he did tell them, resulted in blanks in the family history. The only official written record of Joseph's mother's name was that of Josephine given by his son John at the time of Joseph's death. This is clearly a corruption of and close to the name recorded in Flemish (Dutch) at the time in Joseph's birth, i.e. Joanna Sarah, and perhaps to her English name of Jane Sarah. Perhaps Joseph just couldn't remember accurately. After all he would never have met his English grandmother or Belgian grandfather and it would have had a little meaning to him. And evidently Joseph himself, felt closer to his former school friends than his parents family whom he likely never knew.

Chapter 4

LIFE AFTER SEDGLEY PARK SCHOOL

In the years immediately following young Joseph's leaving school in late 1829 or 1830, little is known prior to his arriving in New Zealand about 1835. It is not known if Joseph kept in touch with his birth family as there are no records to be found. It is unlikely.

Collected anecdotal evidence, mainly the recollections of his family descendants suggests he arrived in New Zealand at a very early age. That seems to be confirmed. If Joseph arrived in 1835, just five years after he left school, that would mean he was thirteen years old. That is close to the recollection of his granddaughter May Hogg[24].

How Joseph arrived in New Zealand is a matter of some conjecture. Some theories suggest he arrived via North America but there is no definite evidence or any data which might go some way to confirming this. Joseph

---

[24] See notes in Annex.

would have had to arrive by ship from any one of many ports which carried on trade with or via New Zealand in the 1830's. At that young age he very possibly had been hired as a young cabin boy which was common at the time. In the absence of any concrete data, it could also be speculated that Joseph possibly arrived in New Zealand as a cabin boy in the Royal Navy or possibly even the French Navy. Young boys were often recruited into the Navy at an early age, often placed there by their families so they gained experience and rose quickly up the ladder and received promotions based on experience. Whatever the case, at that young age young possibly Joseph jumped ship. This could also have been in Sydney from where he would have joined one of the many ships which were crossing the Tasman regularly at that period including to trade with the Bay of Islands and Hokianga.

Given the strong emphasis on the francophone heritage attributed to Joseph, another possible and very speculative theory is that Joseph arrived with Baron De Thierry[25], a Frenchman who arrived in New Zealand in 1837. De Thierry who was educated at Cambridge, knew of New Zealand from his meetings with Hongi Hika who visited Cambridge in 1820 at which time he assisted Professor Samuel Lee who was writing the first Māori–English dictionary. As a result and ultimately to no avail, De Thierry had developed and set about implementing ideas of setting up his own sovereign state in New Zealand with himself as Head of State. Other sources may be consulted to understand the full story of the colourful adventures of De Thierry in New Zealand and his legacy.

It has also been said that there was some link between Joseph and his family with Napoleon. This could very well have been not the Napoleon of French Revolutionary times, but Napoleon III, another failed

---

[25] Charles Philippe Hippolyte de Thierry (April 1793 – 8 July 1864).

French revolutionary who had exiled himself to England in 1835.

Another popular but unlikely theory concerning the relationship to Emperor Napoleon suggests that young Joseph was the son of one of the first Emperor Napoleon's high ranking French cavalry officers, General Jean-Pierre-Joseph Bruguière or Bruyères[26]. Bruyères was on three occasions appointed Aid de Camp to Marechal Louis-Alexandre Berthier, Napoleon's Chef d'Etat Major. In 1810 Bruyères married Joséphine-Thérèse-Virginie the sixteen year old second daughter of Berthier's brother Louis-Cesar-Gabriel. Bruyères and Joséphine-Thérèse had two children, a girl, Jeromia-Catherine born in 1811, and then a son Jean-Pierre-Joseph-Alexandre born on the 28th October 1813, a few months after his father's death on the 15th June 1813. There are no records of any other children[27]. Subsequently in 1830, Joséphine-Thérèse-Virginie married William Thomas the 3rd Baron Graves an English gentleman ten years her junior.

Other theories[28] suggest the Bryers family were involved in the shipping business in Liverpool but that cannot be confirmed. There were a very few families with the name Bryers in Liverpool in the very early part of the nineteenth century with some in shipping and the merchant trade but no indication or evidence at all they were related to the New Zealand Bryers. It is possible that André Joseph Bryers was active as a trader in Liverpool but his centre of activity was on the continent as has been recounted in earlier Chapters. The story is more than likely a mixing up Joseph's origins with those of his son George who definitely did spend some time at Liverpool arriving

---

[26] https://www.napoleon-series.org/research/commanders/c_bruyere.html

[27] Confirmed by private correspondence with Terry J. Senior, author of the series documenting Napoleon's generals and other researchers.

[28] See notes in Annex.

there as a seaman via New Orleans in the United States in 1865. George married a lady called Mary Heron[29] on the 24th July 1865 at St Peter's Chapel, a Catholic Church at Seel Street, Liverpool prior to returning to New Zealand with his young wife.

Later in life, Joseph Bryers demonstrated himself to be completely at home with the sea even if there were eventually several tragedies in his own family as a result of seagoing ventures[30].

Of young Joseph's parents André Joseph and Jane Bryers there are traces of Jane later in the century including at least two sisters of the young Joseph Bryers. By 1851, Jane Bryers was recorded in the census as a widow visiting a Mr William Amies and his wife Ann living at 3 Wansford Place in the St. Pancras Marylebone district of London. Marylebone was a fashionable residential suburb north of Oxford Street, London, established during the late 18th and early 19th centuries[31].

Of interest and at the residence next door to Jane Bryers at number 2 Wansford Place, the home of a Mr. George Packer and his wife Mary, were living Jane's daughters Eliza Bryers born in 1834 at Antwerp, Belgium and Adele Bryers born in 1839 at Paris, France. It is supposed that both were daughters of André Joseph Bryers and Jane although no birth records can be found to confirm this. Both daughters were recorded as dressmakers while the heads of household in each case were stationers and booksellers. The relationship between all these people is unclear from the census data, however it appears they were related by marriage and there may have been another

---

[29] This could have been Heran, Herrin or Herron. As both partners were illiterate or semi-litterate, the accurate spelling of the name remains unknown.

[30] See Chapter 5.

[31] Information from the Society for Promoting Christian Knowledge, the current occupiers of the Parish Church of Marylebone.

Bryers daughter among them. No trace can be found of any date or place of death of André Joseph Bryers, however based on the birth place of his daughters, young Joseph's sisters, it could have been anywhere from Paris to Antwerp and places in between. It was almost certainly not in England[32].

As to Jane Bryers, mother to young Joseph Bryers, death records indicate a lady of that name having passed away in the district of St Pancras on the 2nd November 1880. In all probability this is the lady who gave birth to Joseph Bryers in Ostend, Belgium in 1822. At the time of her death, Jane had clearly fallen on hard times as she was an inmate at the St. Pancras Workhouse and according to her death certificate had died of 'senile decay'. A workhouse was an early form of social support for destitute people and generally an institution to be avoided unless necessary. Although food, lodging and some work was provided, life was extremely regimented and families were split into female and male parts of the institution. The Pancras Workhouse was one of the largest in England at the time. In 1881, the census records some one thousand nine hundred inmates.

It seems that if this was the Jane Bryers, the mother of Joseph, that she had been abandoned by the rest of her family, much as she seems to have abandoned young Joseph all those years ago. In any case, it is almost certain that Joseph Bryers in New Zealand was not aware of her death.

On the 25th March 1860, the sister of Joseph Bryers Junior, Miss Adele Bryers whose name was recorded as Briers in the Church Registry, was married at Trinity Church in the parish of Marylebone to a Mr. Richard

---

[32] A burial of a Joseph Briers is recorded at St John the Baptist Anglican Church at Chipping Barnet in England, just north of London in 1840 however this person was born in 1812 and therefore very definitely not André Joseph Bryers.

Jackson. Adele's father recorded as Joseph Charles Briers[33], a merchant, was recorded as deceased. Mr Jackson, a butcher living at Queen's Terrace, Marylebone, was listed as the son of William Jackson, a surgeon. This demonstrates the fluid interchange of the use of the two forms of the name Bryers and Briers in the family and which had led to so much difficulty in interpreting names over the years. It is unlikely Joseph Bryers in New Zealand was aware of the marriage of his sister.

On the 29th December 1860, Adele Jackson as she was now known, at her address at 15 Mornington Crescent, Pancras, gave birth to a daughter Fanny Adele Eugenie Jackson. The occupation of the father, Richard Jackson, was recorded this time as 'Farmer', a rather strange employ for someone living in London, even if at the time it was the outskirts.

No further traces of any of the family in England have been found going forward and as far as is known, no contact between Joseph Bryers in New Zealand and his English or Belgian families was ever taken up.

---

[33] Just why Adele chose to name her father as Joseph Charles, the name of her brother, remains an unsolved mystery and simply adds to the confusion in sorting out this very complicated family.

The Marylebone Holy Trinity Church where Adele Briers (Bryers) married Richard Jackson on the 25th March 1860 - View c. 1840 from the Outer Circle of Regent's Park. Source: Alamy

Chapter 5

EARLY LIFE IN NEW ZEALAND

It was not the purpose of this account to develop a biography of Joseph Bryers' life in New Zealand. Being one of the early European settlers in the Far North where there was early and deep integration with the indigenous Maori community, Bryers and his fellow Europeans of the day have been the subject of much historical and social study. With its geographical isolation at the end of a long peninsula north of Auckland and relatively limited access, even in modern-day New Zealand, the Far North remains somewhat separate and remains an active area of study as many traditions and practices developed nearly two hundred years ago are still in place.

Studies of the early history of the Far North have tended to focus on the community as a whole and there have been few detailed biographies of individuals. The works of Jack Lee[34] and Ruth Ross[35] immediately come to mind. Then there is the excellent series called the Kaihu River Valley History[36] available on-line and pulled together by Roger Mold. Also available is a plethora of Parliamentary and other reports and many archival documents available in New Zealand Libraries and Museums including that of the Hokianga Historical Society[37], for those with the time and inclination to delve through them.

Concerning Joseph Bryers himself, to the knowledge of the author, probably the best is the family history document written by Judith Holloway[38] for the reunion of the family of Charles Bryers in 1987. Charles, great-grandfather of the author, was the youngest son of Joseph Bryers.

The author cannot better Judith Holloway's account and for the purposes of the present work, it is perhaps useful to provide a short summary of what is known about Joseph Bryers.

The best estimates are that Joseph arrived in New Zealand between 1835 and 1837 as a fair-haired, blue-eyed, young man and probably at the Bay of Islands. At the time 'The Bay' had a reputation for being a pretty much wild and lawless place. Undoubtedly, the country at the time not having any form of modern government or administration,

---

[34] For example: *Hokianga*, Jack Lee, Raupo Publishing (NZ) Ltd, new edition 2006, ISBN 9780790005225; *I Have Named it the Bay of Islands*, Hodder & Stoughton, 1983, ISBN 0 340 338784; *An Unholy Trinity, Three Hokianga Characters,* Jack Lee, Northland Historical Publications Society Incorporated, 1997, ISBN 095979266X.

[35] See http://www.nzjh.auckland.ac.nz/docs/1982/NZJH_16_2_16.pdf

[36] https://kaihuvalleyhistory.com/

[37] Hokianga Historical Society, Waianga Place, Omapere, South Hokianga.

[38] The Bryers family : An account of the beginnings of a Maori-Pakeha family in New Zealand, Judith Holloway, 1993, The Bryers Family, ISBN 0473017628, copies available from Judith Holloway.

there were elements who took great advantage at the lack of any sort of policing. Nevertheless besides the local Maori population who adhered mostly to their own traditional ways and rules, there were European residents who behaved reasonably, but not always respectfully, including many missionaries. One of the earliest and most complete accounts by a European of New Zealand and the Bay of Islands was by Augustus Earle in describing his travels there during 1827[39]. Earle, an English gentleman artist and adventurer did not cast a too favourable light on his fellow Europeans and opined that many exercised a demoralising influence on the local Maori population. Extracts from Earle's account include: *I found a respectable body of Scotch mechanics settled here, who came out in the New Zealand Company's ship Rosanna, and who determined to remain at Kororareka. Their persevering industry as yet has been crowned with success, and they seem well pleased with the prospects before them.*

Here, these hardy sons of Britain are employed in both carrying on and instructing the wondering savage in various branches of useful art. Here the smith has erected his forge, and his sooty mansion is crowded by curious natives, who voluntarily perform the hardest and most dirty work, and consider themselves fully recompensed by a sight of his mysterious labours, every portion of which fills them with astonishment. Here is heard daily the sound of the sawpit, while piles of neat white planks appear arranged on the beach. These laborious and useful Scotchmen interfere with no one, and pursue successfully their industrious career, without either requiring or receiving any assistance from Home.

But there is another class of Europeans here, who are both useless and dangerous, and these lower the character of the

---

[39] *A Narrative of a Nine Months' Residence in New Zealand in 1827* by Augustus Earle, Whitcombe & Tombs Limited, New Zealand, 1909.

white people in the estimation of the natives. These men are called "Beach Rangers," most of whom have deserted from, or have been turned out of whalers for crimes, for which, had they been taken Home and tried, they would have been hanged; some few among them, having been too lazy to finish the voyage they had begun, had deserted from their ships, and were then leading a mean and miserable life amongst the natives.

There is still a third class of our countrymen to be met with here, whose downcast and sneaking looks proclaim them to be runaway convicts from New South Wales. These unhappy men are treated with derision and contempt by all classes; and the New Zealanders, being perfectly aware of their state of degradation, refuse all intercourse with them. They are idle, unprincipled, and vicious in the extreme, and are much feared in the Bay of Islands; for when by any means they obtain liquor, they prove themselves most dangerous neighbours."

Of most interest to the present work are the accounts Earle gives of his encounters with someone he referred to as Shulitea or 'King George'. In reality Shulitea or Te Whareumu[40] was the ariki and warrior chief of Ngāti Manu, a hapū within the Ngāpuhi iwi based in the Bay of Islands and was the most important chief in the Kororakeka area in his day. He was a warrior chief of the highest mana in pre-European times and well respected by the early missionaries and traders, to whom he provided the greatest protection. Te Whareumu had quickly realised the advantage of trading with the many ships visiting the Bay[41].

---

[40] Te Whareumu or 'King George' (circa 1775–1828) born into a high ranking family, was the son of Te Arahi and Te Ruru. He was closely related to Te Ruki Kawiti and Pōmare I (also called Whetoi) and related to most of the northern chiefs. Te Whareumu assumed control of the tribe after the passing of Tara.

[41] https://en.wikipedia.org/wiki/Te_Whareumu

Old Pa and Whalers at the Bay of Islands in A Narrative of a Nine Months' Residence in New Zealand in 1827
by Augustus Earle.   Source: Collection, The Author

Te Whareumu was none other than the father of Kohu Katerina Whareumu who eventually Joseph Bryers was to take as his wife. Earle knew Te Whareumu well and lived with him under his protection and states in his narrative that he was *"On terms of the closest intimacy, and with his hut adjoining that of my friend Captain Duke".....* *"We all felt grateful to him for his manifestations of friendship, and at the same time were conscious of enjoying a greater degree of security by his proximity"*.

However a great tragedy happened to Te Whareumu during Earle's time at the Bay of Islands, an account of which he gives in great detail in his book. In summary, Te Whareumu and his younger brother Kiwikiwi another key member of Ngāpuhi's southern alliance led a taua to Waimā, Hokianga, to avenge the death of Ariki[42], the only son of Pōmare I. Te Whareumu was killed, and it was decided that Kiwikiwi would succeed him. Although he was a leading rangatira, it is said Kiwikiwi did not have the same maturity and experience as Te Whareumu, and his influence was eventually overshadowed by Pōmare II. Earle recounts *"The night before they started on this expedition, George spent the evening with us. He was in particularly low spirits, and said he did not at all like the business he was going upon: but, as he was the nearest relation of the deceased, and the eldest of the tribe, he went in hopes of being able to prevent a great effusion of blood, and also to restrain the impetuosity of the young men. Little did we then think he would be the first victim; although his unusual depression of mind brought to my remembrance the prophecy of Hongi, and, spite of my endeavours to banish my forebodings, I felt convinced that the prediction would in all probability be fulfilled"*.

---

[42] 'Tiki' in Earles' account.

The Bay of Islands in Voyage de la corvette l'Astrolabe exécuté par ordre du roi, pendant les années 1826-1827-1828-1829, Paris, 1833. Source: Courtesy New York Public Library

Throughout all the eventual fighting and skirmishing, during a lull, a woman from the Waima camp was killed by one of Te Whareumu's arms. This in turn led to a new outbreak of fighting during which Te Wahreumu was killed. Earle writes *"Almost at the beginning of the combat George received a shot, which broke both his legs: his brother and friends endeavoured to support him in their arms. It being then nearly dark, added much to the confusion, as it was difficult to distinguish friend from foe; indeed, so sudden had been the onset, that many could scarcely have been aware of the cause of the contest. But our unhappy friend, who seemed particularly marked out in this unfortunate affray, soon after received another bullet, which struck him on the throat, and terminated his existence; thus dying before a week had passed since the death of his rival Hongi"*.

As a consequence of all the bloodshed, Earle and his European companions became fearful for their own lives as a result of the loss of their 'protector'. And within Earle's summary of the conclusion of the affair, there is evidence that Earle was helped by Kohu Katerina Whareumu, Jospeh Bryers' eventual wife. *"Whether the account they gave of themselves was correct, or the reverse, we knew not at the time; but we felt assured their intentions were not hostile towards us Europeans, and their quarrels with each other we were determined not to interfere in. We soon discovered their falsehood, for George's eldest daughter[43] informed me that amongst the chiefs who landed with us were several of the most inveterate foes of her father, and that they were only restrained from committing the most dreadful outrages, and carrying off all her relations as slaves, by witnessing the many friends of George by whom they were surrounded. The day was spent in savage dancing, yelling, making*

---

[43] Almost certainly Kohu Katerina.

speeches, and debating as to who the proper person was to succeed George in his dignities: several times I thought the affair would end in blows. George's relation, Rivers, made great exertions "to keep the peace," and finally, by force of argument, succeeded. It was at length unanimously agreed that Kiney Kiney[44] was to succeed his brother, and that Rivers should take the command until the time of Kiney Kiney's mourning for the loss of George should be completed". Te Whareumu's people continued to associate with the European traders, Earle left New Zealand later in 1827 and life returned to normalcy.

The Bay of Islands in the 1830's was a place where 'one grew up quickly'. The young Joseph had arrived later in the decade and would have met and associated with the many other Europeans at the Bay. Many of those men were having a good time on leave from tough and long whaling trips far from their home ports on the other side of the world and away from supervision. Included among those with whom Joseph associated was a Captain James Norris who was reputed to have taken up with the beautiful Maori girl called Katerina Kohu or Ka Kohu, the daughter of the deceased chieftain Te Whareumu and his wife Moehuri Whareumu. Ka Kohu was thus the descendant of several powerful and respected northern chiefs: Te Whareumu, Kawhiti, and Mohi Tawhai[45]. There are some claims the couple were married according to Christian traditions. When Captain Dillon who was already married left The Bay, there was some competition amongst the remaining seamen at the Bay for the charms of Ka Kohu. Joseph alluded to this many years later when speaking with journalist Lynn Craw[46] in 1883. Joseph recalled *"she (Katerina Ka Kohu) was a fine woman more than forty*

---

[44] Chief Kiwikiwi.

[45] Judith Bryers Holloway, *Rawene News*, 13 August 2020.

[46] The article was published some fifteen years later in the *Southland Times* of 14 March 1898.

years ago and I had a hard fight to get her". Included in the potential suitors was Captain James Norris who had also departed the Bay. It is said that Joseph and Ka Kaho were subsequently married although no marriage record has ever been located. Nevertheless, the eldest child of Joseph Ka Kohu and taken in by Joseph, was called James Norris Bryers. So it was very evident who the father was[47]. Joseph's generosity may have been linked to his own experiences of being abandoned as a child.

Painting by Augustus Earle of a beautiful young Maori girl painted circa 1827 and which is reputed by some to be that of Ka Kohu Katerina Whareumu. Source:Alamy.

---

[47] Judith Holloway, *op. cit.*

Joseph and Ko Kahu moved to the Hokianga where they raised eight children as follows (birth years are estimated as at the time there was no reliable and systematic government recording at the time):

James Norris (Kiwikiwi) – born May 1837 (estimated from death record); died 10 August 1881.
Joseph – born 1840; died November 1865[*]
George – born 1842; died 1911
Matthew – born 1843; died November 1865[*]
John – born 1844; died 3rd September 1934
William- born 1847; died November 1865[*]
Charles – born 1849; died 11th May 1924
Mary Josephine – born 1855; died 1935

[*]*Although most records say Joseph, Matthew and William died in 1866, it was likely to have been November 1865.*

The young Bryers family were great voyagers and there are many records of them visiting Sydney and even further afield.

Throughout his lifetime, Joseph had many employments including as a storekeeper at Herd's Point (Rawene), a hotelkeeper in the same town and as a sea captain in the 1860's with his boat, the schooner 'Kiwi' of 36 tons. The 'Kiwi' was employed as a trading vessel around the coast of New Zealand which as Captain Bryers he ended up knowing exceedingly well and provided many an adventure. The comings and goings of the 'Kiwi' were regularly to be recorded in newspapers accounts of vessel movements all around the country.

DIRECT FOR THE GREY RIVER GOLD DIGGINGS.

THE fast Clipper Schooner 'KIWI,' Captain JOSEPH BRYERS, Master (who is thoroughly acquainted with the coast), will sail on WEDNESDAY next, the 22nd March.

For freight or passage, apply on board, now lying alongside Queen street Wharf.

Captain Joseph Bryers, advertisement for transport to the Grey River gold diggings on the South island, Daily Southern Cross (Auckland), 18 March 1865

In 1866, the schooner 'Kiwi' was to be the source of the greatest tragedy in Joseph's life. In January 1866, The New Zealand Herald (Auckland)[48] reported: *"We regret to learn that fears are entertained for the safety of the schooner Kiwi, Captain Bryers, of Hokianga. Mr, Bryers' two sons (Charles and John), who arrived in the Manukau on Thursday last by the Miranda, from the Grey River, report that the Kiwi sailed from Greymouth, with pasengers for the Manukau over two months ago, since which time nothing has been seen or heard of her. We sincerely hope that the missing craft will ere long give some account of herself."* The Kiwi had arrived at the Grey River from the Hokianga with a cargo of 100 pigs on the 7th November 1865. The timing of her return departure for the Hokianga is unknown but it can have been only a few days later. On the 21st November, the Kiwi was reported in Auckland as being expected back from the Grey River. Following her non-arrival fears, for the fate of the Kiwi along with the three brothers Joseph Jr., Matthew and Willam Bryers and their passengers intensified. Brothers

---

[48] *The New Zealand Herald*, 27 January 1866

John and Charles Bryers had travelled to the South Island and left the Grey River for the return journey to the Manukau on the 18th January 1866[49]. It has to be assumed that Charles and John had visited the South Island in an attempt to determine the fate of their three brothers. There is no record of the fate of the Kiwi ever being accounted for or any wreckage recovered. It was assumed she had been a victim of fierce storms in the vicinity of Cook Strait which had been recorded at the time.

After a long and busy life, Joseph passed away at Rawene in 1885 and he is buried in the family plot in a prominent position in the town cemetery. His wife Ka Kohu it is stated, passed away in 1892 however it is not known with any certainty where she is buried. In any case even though space was provided, there is no record of her being buried alongside her husband in the Rawene town cemetery.

---

[49] *Daily Southern Cross* (Auckland), 26 January 1866.

Chapter 6

CONCLUSIONS

It would be almost an exaggeration to say that Joseph Bryers did not have a gilded start in life. He seems to have recalled very little and perhaps this was a very deliberate action. He had been abandoned by his parents - a father who was almost twice as old as his mother and who was on his second marriage and spent much of the period when Joseph was very young, avoiding the clutches of the law.

Such abandonment was not uncommon for children at the time, especially amongst the monied and upper classes. It is highly likely that many of the other boys at Sedgley Park, the school Joseph attended, were in a similar situation. In any case, Joseph in later life apparently regarded the school and the boys he had known there as his closest approximation to a family. That was until he was able in time to raise his own children.

It is now obvious that young Joseph's life experience was severely disrupted with almost no family links and he had to very quickly grow to a young man with little guidance except that from his schooling.

It is an interesting proposition to pose the question as to what was Joseph's nationality. To begin to answer this question accurately, it is useful to have some historical background.

Europe and especially the area of the Low Countries were in much turmoil in the early nineteenth century. Within that, the history of Belgium before the creation of the modern state in 1830 is intertwined with those of its neighbours: the Netherlands, Germany, France and Luxembourg. Early on, what is now Belgium was part of a larger Empire later, divided into a number of smaller states such as the Duchy of Brabant, the County of Flanders and the Prince-Bishopric of Liège. Because of its physical location between different countries and cultures, Belgium is often referred to as the 'crossroads of Europe' and the 'battlefield of Europe' as a result of the many armies which have fought on its soil. The modern country even today is divided by a language barrier between the Latin French and the Germanic Dutch.

Belgium's modern territory can be in some measure traced from the lands of 'Seventeen Provinces' of the Burgundian Netherlands which straddled the frontier which separated medieval France and Germany. Later they were unified into one autonomous territory by the heirs of Charles V, the Holy Roman Emperor. The Eighty Years' War (1568–1648) later led to the split between a northern Dutch Republic and the Southern Netherlands from which Belgium and Luxembourg later developed. This southern Netherlands territory was ruled at first by the Habsburg descendants, first as the 'Spanish Netherlands'. Invasions of the troops of Louis XIV of France led to the loss of what is now the Nord-Pas-de-Calais Region to France while the remainder became the 'Austrian Netherlands'. After the French Revolution began in 1789 and the various resulting wars, Belgium became part of France in 1795. With the defeat of Napoleon at Waterloo in Belgium in 1815 the new United Kingdom of the Netherlands was created which eventually split again during the Belgian Revolution of 1830 leading to the three nations of today, Belgium, the Netherlands, and Luxembourg.

To Joseph's nationality then. The question of nationality is complex and difficult to answer and is to a large extent irrelevant. In today's terms Joseph would be classified as a Belgian and within that, Flemish. However, as Belgium as a country did not come into existence until 1830 and prior to that and at the time of Joseph's birth in 1822, Belgium was part of the Kingdom of the Netherlands. Thus Joseph might be considered to be born in the Netherlands. His father was possibly born in the francophone region, i.e. French-speaking region of Wallonia around Liège but probably of Dutch-speaking parents. Certainly Joseph Bryers senior was present in and commercially active in Liège from around 1800 and besides French, almost certainly spoke Dutch and English as well. It should be noted that the upper classes tended to speak French whatever their origins. The name Briers is most common in the Dutch-speaking part of Belgium and particularly to the south of the modern city of Antwerp around Herselt[50]. Joseph's father's first wife appears to have been from a Dutch-speaking region, probably Mechelen in todays' Antwerp Province though the family lived and brought up their children in French-speaking Liège. Thus Joseph's immediate family probably spoke Dutch, French and English for as long as Joseph was part of it however it was never a 'French' family.

Did Joseph's start in life affect the way affect the way Joseph conducted himself in later years? It is almost certain that it played some role as revealed in an article

---

[50] The author living in Belgium for nearly fifty years, often encountered the name 'Briers', particularly in Dutch-speaking regions and had long wondered if there was any family connection.

entitled 'A summer Ramble in the Far North' published in the Southland Times[51] by Lynn Craw in 1898 and recounting the adventures of a trip Lynn had made 15 years previously. The second part of his account Craw had written of his encounter with Joseph Bryers in old age at Herd's Point[52] was just prior to Joseph passing away. The quote from Craw's story is revealing and probably is reflective of Joseph's personal philosophy, quite possibly based on his early life experiences. *"In the course of the afternoon Mr Bryers asked me to take a walk and see his garden which was in the old part of the town, and which I saw was his favourite hobby. The fruit was very fine as also the vegetables. 'This is where I live', he said, pointing to the house. 'It was the first hotel and I don't care to shift my quarters now to the new one: money is of no consequence to me and never was much; I wouldn't alter my style of life to please any one if I had tons of gold.'"*

A fitting end to this account.

---

[51] *Southland Times*, 14 March 1898.
[52] Modern day Rawene.

Annex:

A random collection of personal and written accounts of family stories and letters as to the origin of Joseph Bryers.

These accounts (mostly extracts and observations) have been collected by the author over the years from various sources. Where known, the authors and sources are acknowledged. Note: The extracts and quotes assembled are by no means claimed to be exhaustive.

Waldo Heap[53] Collected Manuscipts, Auckland Museum Library MS 132: Letter May Hogg née Bryers (daughter of John Bryers, son of Joseph Bryers)[54] to Waldo Heap, 29 March 1965.

> *"My father's history is or could be very interesting for his father was a fair blue eyed Frenchman & his name was really De Briers and his father was a great linguist & was with Napoleon to the end as interpreter.*
>
> *My father's, father & his mother fled from France to England during the revolution & his mother was housekeeper to some Archbishop & Grandpa used to ride in Sedgeley Park. Then as a boy of 12 he came to N.Z. & when he went back to see his mother she had gone over to "Chicago" so he could find no trace of her. She may have perished in the fires raging there. So be it...."*

---

[53] Waldo Arthur Heap (1907 – 1986) a local historian who specialised in the history of Northland, New Zealand, particularly that of early Northland settlers.

[54] May Hogg passed away on the 8th September 1965 six months after writing this letter.

Waldo Heap Correspondence, Auckland Museum Library MS 132, Box 6, Folio 75: Letter to Ruth Ross[55], 9 December 1962,

> *"August 21st 1852. Joseph Bryers a passenger on the "Moa" from Auckland to Sydney.*
>
> *March the 2nd 1853, J. Bryers a passenger on the "Kirkwood" from Melbourne to Auckland. Also from the same source.*
>
> *November 12th, 1853, Joseph Bryers and Joseph Bryers jun. Passengers for "Herald" from the Bay to Auckland. This looks as though Bryers had another son Joseph probably the eldest who died before his father died."*

Waldo Heap Collected Manuscipts, Auckland Museum Library, Manuscript 132, box 5, Folio 5: Letter from Phillip Wilson to Waldo Heap, 31st of October 1964; and

> *"One point puzzles me. You see that the original Bryers was Joseph, who married Kohu, and that there was a son also called Joseph who died.*
> *However, in Grey's Away in the Far North, he says the father, i.e. Susan's grandfather, is called Jimmy. Could this be correct? And then the Joseph you mentioned as having died could he be the only*

Joseph in the family - or could "Jimmy" be slang for Joseph?"

Waldo Heap Collected Manuscipts, Auckland Museum Library: Manuscript 1325, Box 5 Folio 4 - Letter from Waldo Heap to Phillip Wilson, 9th April 1960

"William Arthur Satchell married Susan Bryers in 1886. However the old Marriage Notice Books contain additional information to that in the Marriage Register. In the Notice Book he is described as "living at Waima, resident 3 years". This suggests that he arrived in New Zealand - if not Waima - about 1883. In Susan Bryers, Satchell married a real New Zealander. Her father Joseph Bryers was born in London about 1816 and arrived in New Zealand about 1835. About 1839 he married, at Russell, Kohu Whareumu, who was probably either the daughter all belong to the family of the well-known Bay of Islands chief Whareumu. No doubt Satchells half caste wife contributed to the understanding of the Maori."

Rawene News, 13th August 2020
Short history of Joseph Bryers by: Judith Bryers Holloway

"Joseph Bryers (originally named Jean-Pierre-Joseph-Alexander Bruyeres) and Kohu Whareumu married (possibly with Maori rites, as the English missionaries refused to officially marry any Maori person who had not been baptised). There are no records but we think they were married by Bishop Pompallier in Russell in 1838.

They were both about 25. Joseph was of French origin (his father had been one of Napoleon's

Cavalry generals who died in battle at Reichenbach in 1813 when Joseph was still in the womb). Calling himself by the English version of his name, Joseph came to NZ first as a 'sawyer' (possibly to construct oil barrels) on a whaling ship, via Mystic Bay on the east coast of America. He met Kohu, the descendant of several powerful and respected northern chiefs – Te Whareumu, Kawhiti, and Mohi Tawhai. She had previously been 'married' to two different ship's captains – Captain Robert Duke and Captain James Norris (but both had wives back home). Joseph said that he had to 'fight for' Kohu. Possibly he had to fight James Norris as he adopted the child Kohu was carrying at the time, naming him James Norris Bryers.

Joseph inherited money when his mother (who had by then married an English Baron) died in 1830 and he built a house and general store and the Masonic Hotel which still stands in Rawene.

Joseph and Kohu had a very happy marriage and produced eight children, several of whom died young from tuberculosis, the curse of early crosscolonisation."

Extract from notes in preparation for the Reunion of the Descendants of Charles Bryers, Author: Judith Holloway.

Attached to notes from Owen Chaney for the Reunion at Avondale, Auckland, 24-25 October 1987.

"Adelaide Bryers, in her evidence to Land Commissioner Bell in 1942, stated:
Joseph Bryers came from England first but via America. He came to NZ in a whaling boat; he was

a shipping man and traded between Sydney and Russell. He came to NZ first somewhere about 1830 or before.

"Joseph Bryers's death certificate (1885) states that he had lived in New Zealand for fifty years and that he was aged 69 in 1885. This means that he was born in 1816 and came to New Zealand to live in 1835. These dates are not necessarily totally accurate.

"The death certificate, signed by his son John, further states that he was born in London and that his father was a military man. His parents' names were Joseph and Josephine.

However, an entry in an old records book in the Rawene Post Office that I perused way back in the early seventies (since destroyed by fire, I believe) said that he came from Liverpool. Of course, he could have been born in London before the family went to live in Liverpool or thereabouts. Or he could simply have left from Liverpool originally in a ship, perhaps sailing to America to sign up on one of the whalers leaving from Fairhaven or Mystic in the state of Massachusetts. This could be a fascinating area of research for anyone particularly interested in whaling history.

"Everything points to the parents being French, and therefore at least nominally Catholic. In order to trace Joseph's birth details, a search will need to be undertaken of Catholic parish registers in London and Liverpool, under Bryers, as well as Brueys and other French possibilities, circa 1816.

"Jean Irvine in TOWNSHIP OF RAWENE states that in the list of 39 Hokianga voters on the first Bay of Islands electorate roll in 1856 was Joseph Bryers' name, the only one in Rawene. There was a property qualification applying and neither Maori nor women could vote. Joseph was listed as a sawyer with a landed estate."

Assembled Bryers Family Records (dated 1971) of John Sidney Baker[56] of Auckland, great grandson of Joseph Bryers

"Joseph Bryers of Liverpool came to New Zealand via North America. Interests in shipping line."

---

[56] John Sidney Baker (1909 – 1983), the author's father.